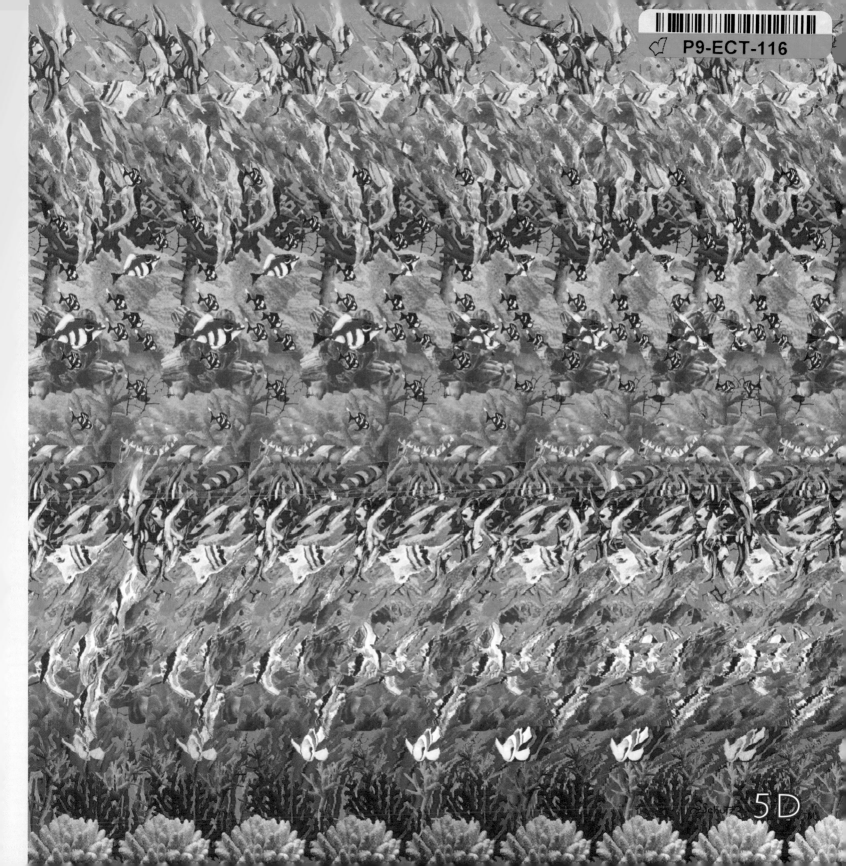

5D

How to See the Hidden 5-D™ Stereogram Image

Hold the art close to your nose so that it appears blurry. Relax your eyes and stare at the artwork. Make believe you are looking "through" the art. Slowly move the artwork away from your face until the hidden Multi-Dimensional image resolves into perfect clarity. The time it takes to see the image can vary, so don't get discouraged!

Alternate viewing method: Place a sheet of plastic or glass over the page so that you can see your own reflection. Hold the art at arm's length and focus on your reflection in the plastic or glass until the 5-D™ stereogram image resolves into perfect clarity.

If you are still unable to see the images, pictures of the hidden 5-D™ stereogram images can be found at the end of this book.

Important: If you experience any discomfort, stop, rest, and try again later.

SEA LIFE
in 5-D™ Stereograms

Created by Stephen Schutz, Ph.D.,
and Susan Polis Schutz

Every illustration in this book
has a hidden 5-D™ stereogram picture
waiting to be discovered by you.

Blue Mountain Press ®

Boulder, Colorado

Five percent of the publisher's proceeds from the sale of
this book is being donated to a nonprofit organization which
supports oceanographic research and education.

This book is printed on recycled paper.

Mail Order

Other exciting 5-D™ products available from Blue Mountain Press:

Greeting Cards

Prints (11" x 14")

Books:

    Endangered Species in 5-D™ Stereograms

    Love in 5-D™ Stereograms

    Reach for Your Dreams in 5-D™ Stereograms

    Sports in 5-D™ Stereograms

Calendars:

    Endangered Species in 5-D™ Stereograms

    Sea Life in 5-D™ Stereograms

    Sports in 5-D™ Stereograms

For ordering information, please contact us at:

Blue Mountain Press
Mail Order
P.O. Box 4549
Boulder, CO 80306
(303) 449-0536

The following people are to be thanked for their valuable contribution to this book:
Faith Gowan, Peter Kay, Patty Brown, Ed Guzik, Mark Rinella, Matt Rantanen, Jared Schutz, Chuck Colgan and the Scripps Institution of Oceanography.

Thanks to the San Diego Museum of Natural History for permission to photograph the penguins used in the 5-D™ stereogram "Emperor Penguin."

ISBN: 0-88396-414-7

Printed in Hong Kong
First Printing: March, 1995

Blue Mountain Press®

P.O. Box 4549, Boulder, Colorado 80306

Introduction

The ocean is home to an amazing diversity of life and mysteries that we are only beginning to understand and explore. Yet our growing awareness and interest come at a time when human activities increasingly threaten the ocean and all its inhabitants. Accidental oil spills and deliberate dumping of garbage and toxic waste stain the waters. Expanding human populations ruthlessly compete with sea life for the ocean's vast food resources. Tens of thousands of marine mammals and turtles, and perhaps millions of birds, are killed annually by commercial ocean fishing. Plankton and other microscopic creatures are dying in record numbers. Destruction of shorelines and pollution of coastal waters threaten the breeding grounds of many species. Clearly, we are at the crossroads in our use of the ocean. Our actions today will decide its eventual fate.

Without the ocean, life on earth could not exist. Covering more than seventy percent of the globe, and containing ninety-seven percent of all the water on earth, the ocean plays a fundamental, defining role in the health of the biosphere. It moderates the world's climate and creates conditions where life can thrive. There is even a miniature ocean within each of us: sixty-five percent of the human body is saltwater. In many ways, the ocean is earth's most important ecosystem, yet we really understand so little about it.

In a spirit of reverence and respect for the life-giving seas, this book celebrates the phenomenal beauty and variety of the ocean's inhabitants and ecosystems. May it also remind us all that we human beings have the ultimate responsibility for ensuring the health of the ocean. It is a legacy not only to our descendants, but to the unborn generations of all the world's creatures. We must take every step necessary to ensure that this legacy is one we can pass on to the future with pride.

Killer Whale (Orca)

Killer whales, found in all the world's oceans, live in communal groups of 4-40 individuals that remain together for life. These groups, or pods, use intricate underwater calls and whistles to communicate, navigate, and hunt. Killer whales are voracious hunters, feeding on a diverse diet of fish, seals, sea turtles, and other whale species. Despite their intimidating name, killer whales have a playful demeanor and have never been known to attack humans. Thankfully, most people see them for what they really are: one of nature's most beautiful creatures.

5-D™ Stereogram Image: **"Mother and Calf"**

Harp Seal

Every spring, thousands of pregnant harp seals congregate in rookeries on the ice of Greenland and Canada, where each gives birth to a single pup. These "whitecoat" pups, as they are often called, have downy white fur that protects them from the Arctic cold and camouflages them on the ice from natural predators. But this magnificent evolutionary adaptation, which had helped thousands of generations of baby seals survive, made them the targets of human hunters who coveted the fur for making winter coats. International outrage over this "harvest," combined with a ban on importing products made from the whitecoat pelts, helped to stop commercial hunting — making the northern rookeries safe once more for harp seal pups and their mothers.

5-D™ Stereogram Image: **"Mother Harp Seal with Her Pup"**

PLAYFUL DOLPHINS
(Surfing)

The human bond with dolphins goes back to ancient times, as their likenesses can be found on early coins and artifacts. The Greek philosopher Aristotle related stories of dolphins befriending children and allowing them to ride on their backs. Dolphins were also said to have saved people from drowning. Unfortunately, pollution now threatens some of their habitats. Thousands of dolphins are killed every year, entangled in the huge nets cast by commercial fishermen. Many nations — including the U.S. — have prohibited importing tuna caught in ways that harm dolphins. This is helping more dolphins than ever to survive and live out their lives in the world's oceans.

5-D™ Stereogram Image: **"Surfing Dolphins"**

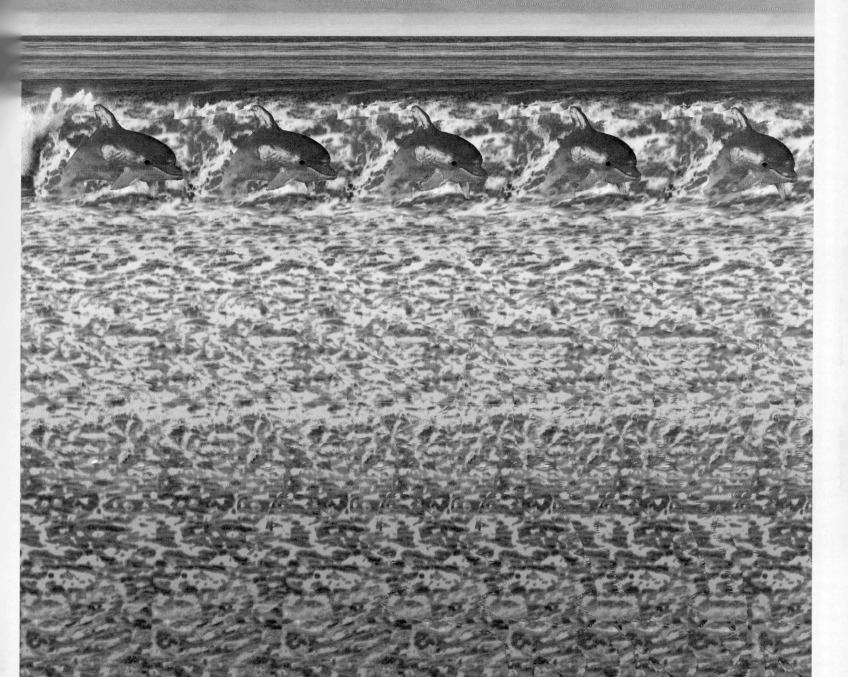

5·D™
SSchutz

HUMPBACK WHALE

A hundred years ago, the haunting song of the humpback whale would resonate through the wooden hulls of whaling ships and fill the sailors with awe and wonder. It is believed that these songs could travel such a great distance that whales hundreds of miles apart could communicate. But technology brought increasingly effective ways of killing whales; in the first four decades of this century, more whales were killed than in the previous four centuries. Today, nearly thirty years after an international ban on hunting humpbacks, there are still only a few thousand alive. It may take many more decades for these magnificent singers of the deep waters to recover in numbers significant enough to hope for any long-term survival.

5-D™ Stereogram Image: **"Diving Humpback Whale"**

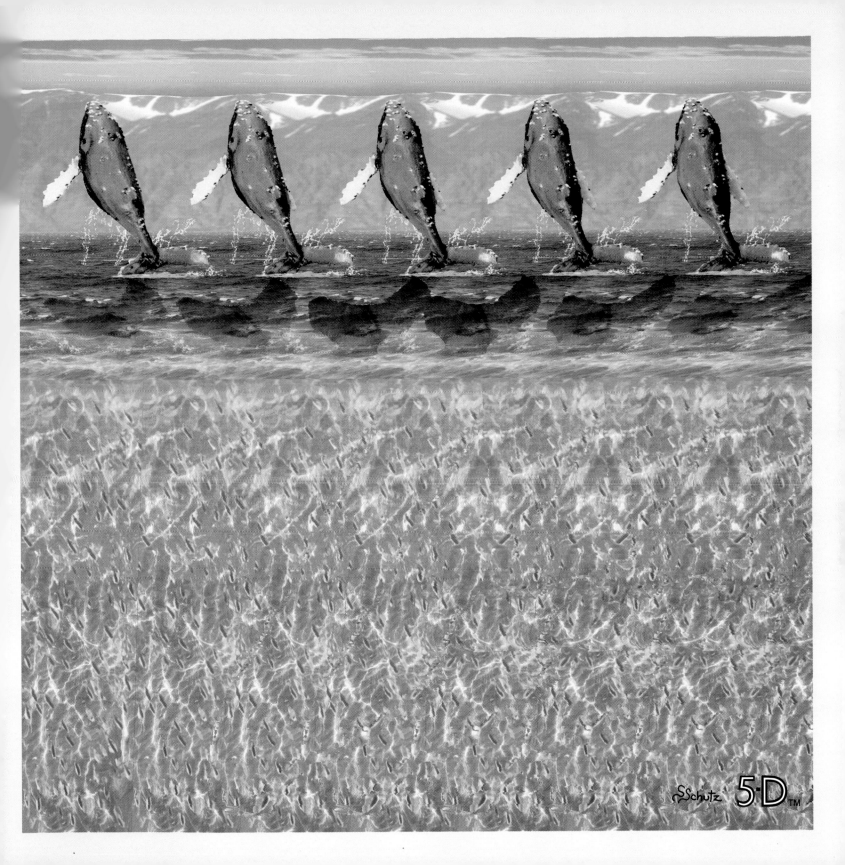

FRIENDLY HARBOR SEAL

Like a sleek, graceful mermaid, a hungry harbor seal speeds through the sea, pirouetting to catch fish in an enchanting underwater ballet. Others "haul out" on the rocks and beaches of sheltered inlets to sun, rest, and play. To most people, these friendly seals are a harmless natural wonder, but to many coastal fishermen, they are unwanted competition. While fishermen once hunted and killed thousands each year, the Marine Mammal Protection Act, passed in 1972, limited such hunting to ensure that the playful harbor seal would remain a common sight in coastal waters. A half a million or more still frolic in the seas of the world.

5·D™
SSchutz

ENDANGERED MANATEE

These gentle, giant herbivores inspired the first legends of mermaids. Today, their endangered status is inspiring people to help them survive as a species. Manatees must overcome both natural and manmade dangers. Significant drops in water temperature can be fatal for manatees, and collisions with powerboats have also killed many of them. In the last few years, programs to breed manatees in captivity and release them into the wild have met with limited success; public awareness of the manatee's situation has somewhat decreased the number of fatal collisions. But shrinking habitats and pollution of their home waters continue to threaten the long-term survival of this peaceful creature.

5-D™ Stereogram Image: **"Manatee with Calf"**

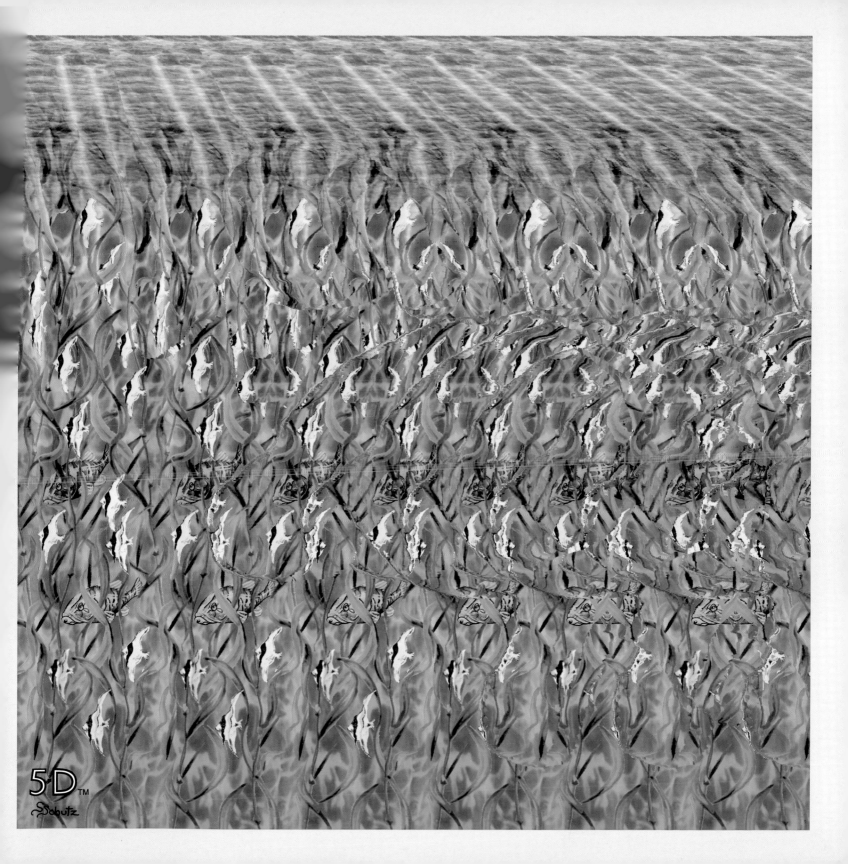

THE SHORELINE

On the boundary between the worlds of land and sea, the shoreline is a
constantly changing environment. It is home to creatures and plants
found nowhere else on earth, as well as a source of food and shelter for
both its year-round residents and migrating animals. Unfortunately, it is
also the most vulnerable and visible indicator of man's degradations in
the oceans — the place where oil spills wash ashore, killing shore life
and seabirds, and where trash and pollution often create unsafe
conditions for the animals who call the shore their only home. Most of
the world's shorelines have been virtually stripped of the larger animals
and seaweeds by human collecting.

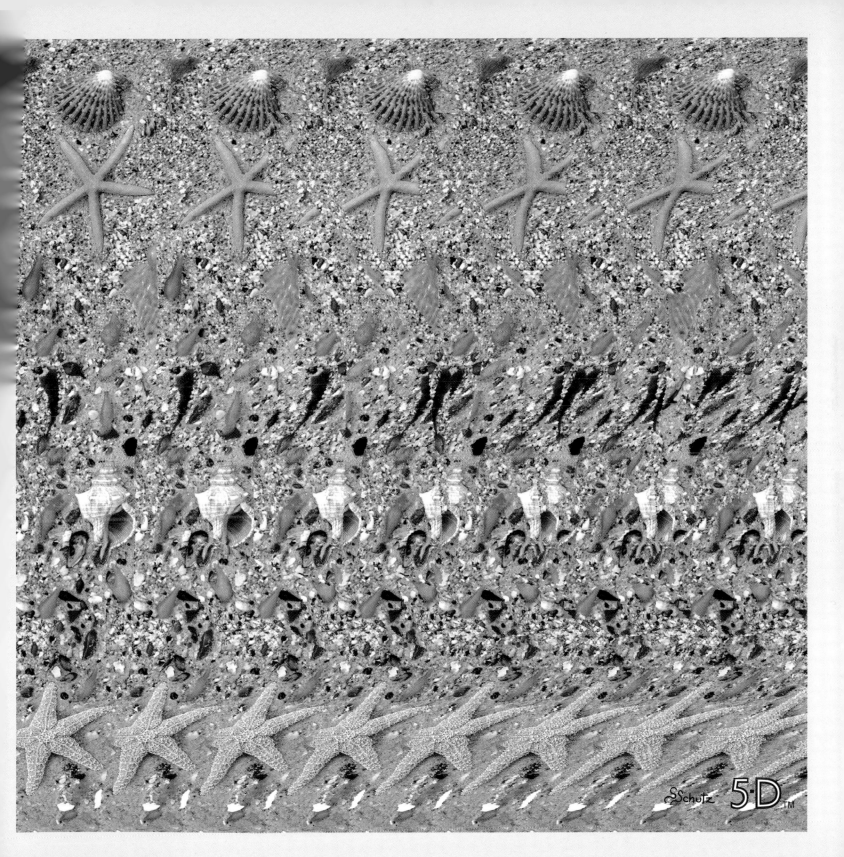

Threatened Arctic Sea Life

Although the frigid sea and ice pack of the Arctic may seem like a desolate wasteland, it is actually a thriving universe filled with some of the most hardy species on earth. Today, commercial fishing and industrialization threaten seas that were once protected from man by their harsh climate. Whaling fleets have depleted seas once filled with whales, leaving populations far smaller than a century ago. Predators such as the polar bear, once king of the Arctic ice pack, must increasingly compete with man for control of its icy kingdom. Highly toxic materials have been dumped into northern seas, and oil exploration threatens once pristine Arctic habitats. Though the Arctic does not often enjoy the publicity and protection of regions like rain forests, it is an equally vital part of our natural world.

5-D™ Stereogram Image: **"Polar Bear Mother and Cub"**

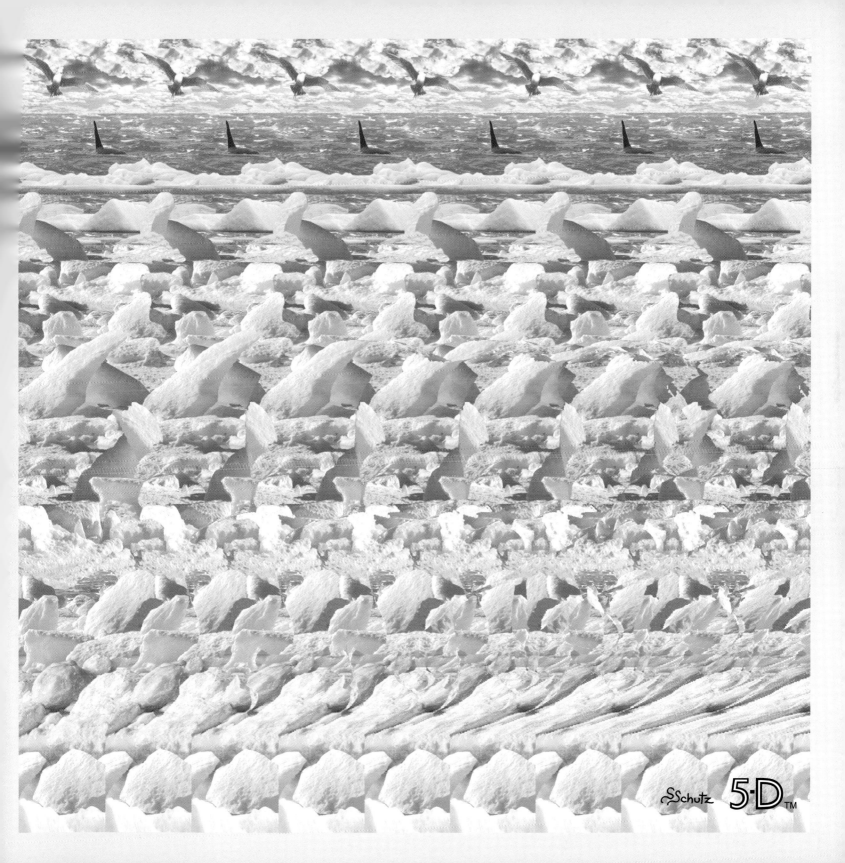

Pacific Sea Life
(Sea Lion and Brown Pelican)

Above the rocky cliffs, sandy beaches, and blue waters of the Pacific, brown pelicans swoop down upon unsuspecting fish, scooping them up in their pouch-like bills. Seals and sea lions frolic in the surf, taking breaks to lounge on the rocks. Thanks to legislation like the Marine Mammal Protection Act and laws restricting DDT insecticide use, threatened species such as the brown pelican have been saved from extinction in Pacific waters. Others, like the California sea lion, have shown substantial population increases, demonstrating that man and animal can coexist on the beautiful Pacific coast. Unfortunately, the populations of other marine mammals, such as the Steller sea lion, continue to decline because of encroachment by humans on their habitats.

THREATENED SEA TURTLES

After surviving 100 million years of evolution, sea turtles seem supremely adapted to any obstacle nature can throw in their path... except man. Sea turtles once filled the world's oceans; now, eight species are either threatened or endangered. Beach resorts encroach upon turtle nesting areas, and fishermen's nets drown an estimated 11,000 to 44,000 each year. Although some sea turtles spend nearly 98 percent of their lives under water, a flailing turtle caught in a fisherman's net can drown within minutes. A substantial number of sea turtles die from eating plastic debris, which they mistake for jellyfish. Concerned environmentalists have encouraged fishermen to use turtle-safe nets and have set aside beaches for nesting, helping sea turtles to survive in an increasingly threatening world. Unfortunately, most refuges still experience severe poaching.

5-D™ Stereogram Image: **"Sea Turtle"**

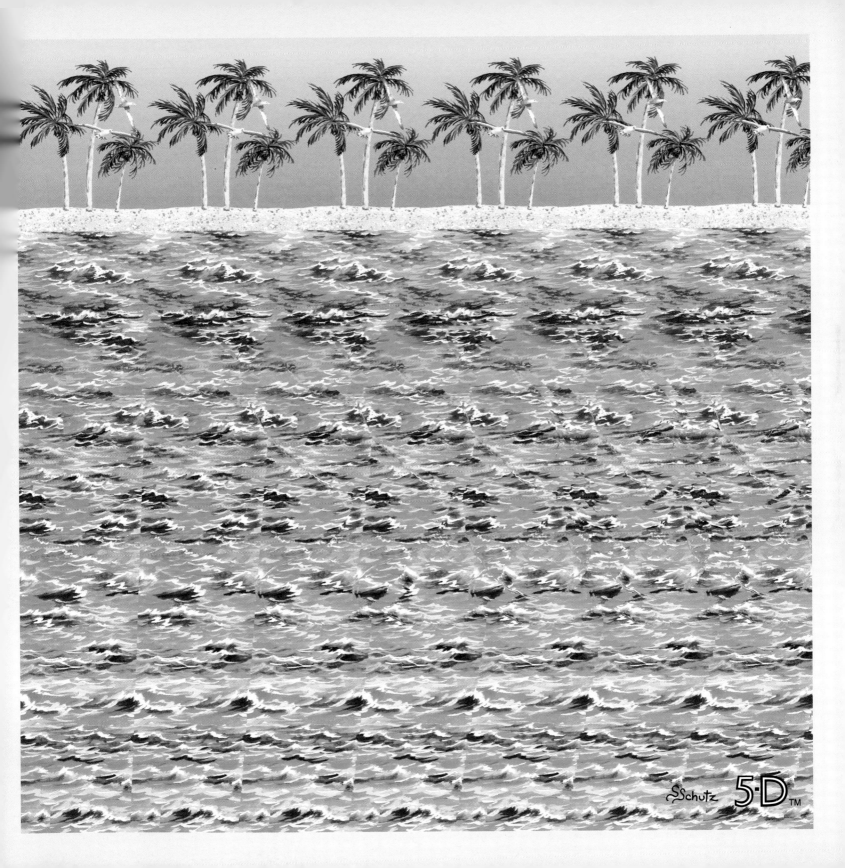

Emperor Penguin

In the perpetual darkness of the Antarctic winter, as many as 100,000 male Emperor penguins congregate together in a single place. For two long months, they survive without food, huddling together for warmth and protection against 100-mph winds and temperatures as low as -40°F. They endure all of this for the sake of the next generation of penguins. As the largest penguin, the Emperor is one of a few species in which the male is solely responsible for incubating the egg. After his partner lays a single egg, the male rolls it onto his feet and covers it with his body. All the females then return to the open sea to hunt. They reunite with the males soon after the eggs have hatched, and both parents participate in rearing their hatchling until summer returns and the young penguins can care for themselves.

5-D™ Stereogram Image: **"Swimming Penguin"**

Great White Shark

Ravenous, fearless, menacing, and above all mysterious, the great white shark can grow to a massive 7,000 pounds and 25 feet in length. This skilled predator uses sensory capabilities as sensitive as manmade sonar to track down prey. Though movies and books have painted an intimidating picture of the great white, the shark very rarely attacks humans. In truth, man presents more of a threat to the shark than the shark does to man, as trophy-seeking fishermen threaten sparse populations. Man's often irrational fears aside, the great white should be appreciated as one of nature's most awe-inspiring creations.

5-D™ Stereogram Image: "Great White"

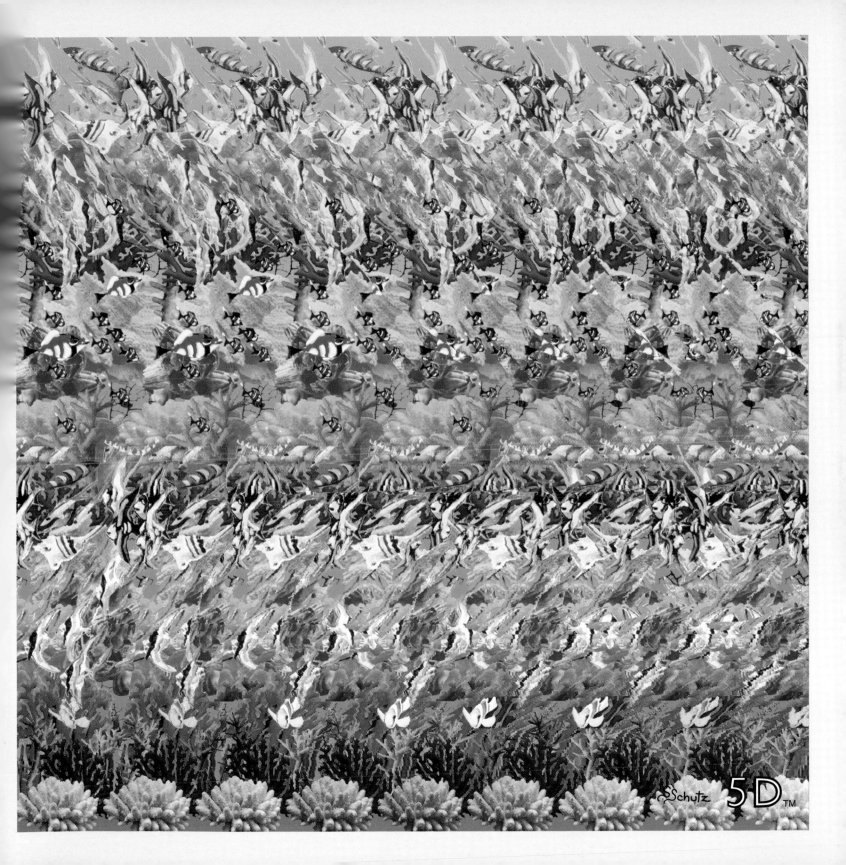

PLAYFUL DOLPHINS
(Jumping)

For centuries, sailors have regarded the presence of dolphins near their ships as a good omen — a promise of smooth sailing and a safe voyage ahead. Today, dolphins are a symbol of the health of the oceans and of humanity's treatment of all wild creatures. Scientists continually discover patterns of behavior and interaction that seem to occur only in dolphins and humans. They are complex, highly sociable animals who hunt and play together; when one is injured or ill, the others help it swim to the surface to breathe. For sixty million years, dolphins have found a haven of safety in the ocean, but that security is now threatened by human exploitation of the seas.

5-D™ Stereogram Image: **"Dolphins"**

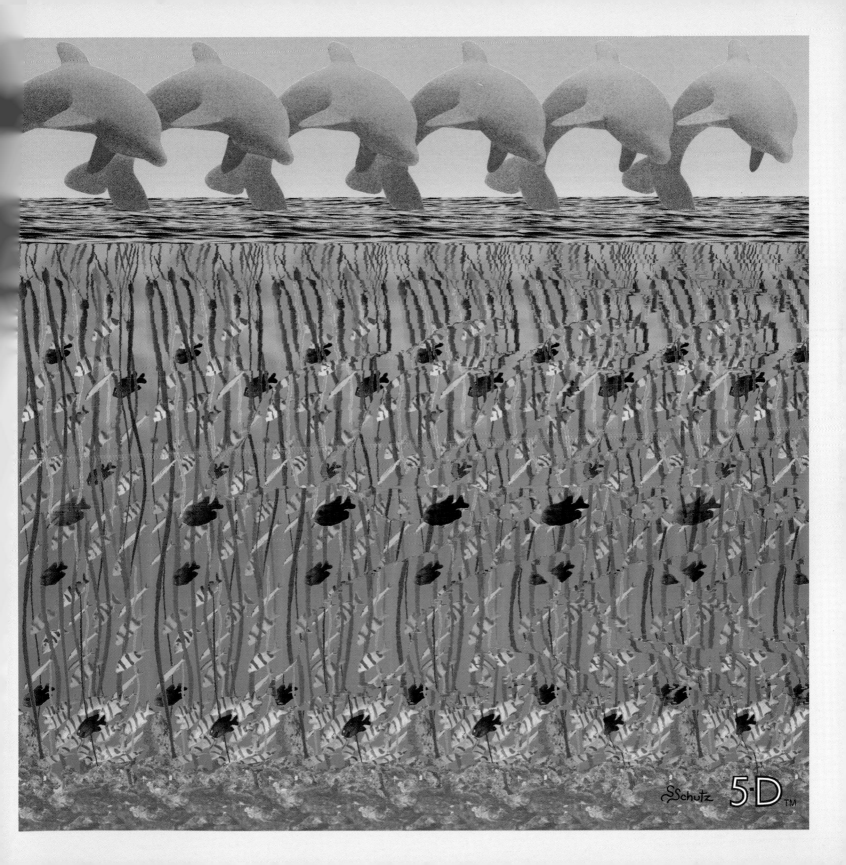

Seeing in Stereo

Stephen Schutz, Ph.D., Takes the Art of the Stereogram to a New Aesthetic Level

Recent improvements in computer technology have enabled the famous artist (and physicist) Stephen Schutz to pass a new threshold of innovation and liberate art from its prior two-dimensional limitations. "Spectacular!" says Leonard Nimoy about 5-D™ stereograms. "Beautiful and often dazzling works of art," says Dick Kreck of *The Denver Post*.

5-D™ stereograms, Stephen Schutz's most recent artistic creation, effectively establish a genre of Multi-Dimensional art. Stereograms had their origins in 1960 when Bela Julesz developed the "random-dot stereogram" as a tool to study perceptual psychology. For the past thirty years, primitive random-dot stereograms have relied on repetitive textures to disguise hidden three-dimensional images.

Stephen Schutz's 5-D™ stereograms have successfully replaced random-dot textures with incredible artwork, which makes 5-D™ stereograms "dimensional dynamite," in the words of David Hutchison of the National Stereoscopic Association. The full-color base-art foregrounds (what everyone sees on the surface) are attractions in and of themselves. When this foreground is dramatically supplemented by a hidden image that relates and interacts with it, the exquisite result comes alive as dolphins leap off the page and pelicans glide through a multi-layered sky. Stephen Schutz's accomplishment is a testimony to what can happen when the creative envelope of art is expanded and enhanced by the cutting edge of technology.

"Over the past few years, random-dot stereograms have been popping up all over the place. Unfortunately, most are very boring," notes 3-D collector and writer for *Stereo World* magazine, Sheldon Aronowitz. "This has all changed with the release of the Blue Mountain Arts 5-D™ stereograms developed by Dr. Stephen Schutz. In their flat format, they are works of art in their own right. When viewed in three dimensions, you will be amazed and delighted with the clarity and ingenious blending of theme. No more patterns of endless dots."

About the Artist and Author

Stephen Schutz is an artist and a physicist, a rare combination of talents emanating from the mind and heart. Enraptured at an early age with beauty and aesthetic form, Stephen pursued the paths of science and art simultaneously. He graduated from the famous High School of Music and Art in New York, and studied physics at M.I.T. and Princeton University, where he received a Ph.D. in theoretical physics in 1970. While pursuing advanced scientific learning, Stephen continued to develop his artistic abilities at the Museum of Fine Arts in Boston.

During college, Stephen met and fell in love with the woman who was to become his equal loving partner in marriage, family, and art. In 1969, Susan Polis Schutz and Stephen Schutz moved to the mountains of Colorado where Susan was a freelance writer and Stephen researched solar energy at a government research laboratory. On the weekends, they began experimenting with printing Susan's poems surrounded by Stephen's art on posters that they silk-screened in their basement. From the very start, their love of life and for one another touched a receptive chord in people everywhere. The public's discovery of the creative collaboration of Susan Polis Schutz and Stephen Schutz set the stage for a world-wide love affair with their works. Frequent visitors to the bestseller lists, Susan and Stephen's books and poetry cards have touched the hearts of over 200 million people, and their works have been translated into many languages.

Because Stephen is an artist, computer whiz, and innovator, there is no one better suited to take the art of the stereogram to its next level. Combine that with the fact that it would be difficult to discover a poet with a more significant following than Susan Polis Schutz, who *TIME* magazine referred to as "the reigning star… in high emotion." Together, Susan and Stephen Schutz's most recent books, featuring Susan's poetic messages and Stephen's 5-D™ stereograms, are just the latest in a series of beautiful contributions the couple has made over the past 25 years.

Hidden 5-D™ Stereogram Images

Mother and Calf

Mother Harp Seal
with Her Pup

Surfing Dolphins

Diving Humpback Whale

Swimming Seal

Manatee with Calf

Sea Gull over Waves

Polar Bear Mother
and Cub

Sea Lion

Sea Turtle

Swimming Penguin

Great White

Dolphins

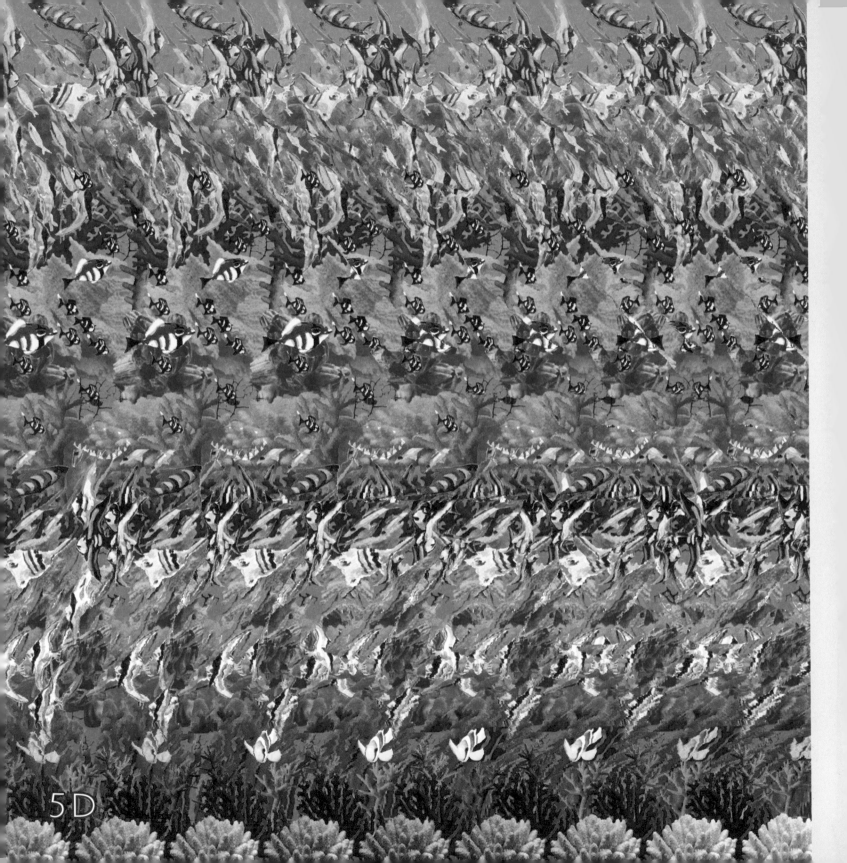